Keeping Track of the Weather

Jill Andersen

Rosen REAL READERS

Rosen Classroom™
New York

Scientists keep track of the weather. They use special tools.

This is a thermometer.

It shows how hot or cold it is.

Scientists use tools
to track the wind.

They use a barometer.

It measures air pressure.

They use a rain gauge.

It measures how much rain falls.

Scientists use satellites.
They track storms.

They use weather balloons, too.

Scientists collect information.

They can tell if it will be
a nice day.

They can warn people
about storms, too.

Words to Know

balloon

barometer

rain gauge

satellite

storm